The 100 Most Confusing
Verses in the Bible

All Books in this Series

The 100 Best Bible Verses on Prayer

The 100 Best Bible Verses on Heaven

The 100 Most Encouraging Verses of the Bible

The 100 Best Bible Verses About Salvation

The 100 Best Bible Verses on Marriage, Family & Parenting

The 100 Most Confusing Verses in the Bible

The 100 Best Verses for Mom

THE 100 MOST CONFUSING VERSES IN THE BIBLE

Troy Schmidt

THE 100 MOST CONFUSING VERSES IN THE BIBLE
(VOLUME 6)

Copyright @ 2018 by Troy Schmidt
All rights reserved
Second edition
Printed November, 2019

Printed in the United States of America

Cover design by David Hicks

For more information about the Author, go to
www.troyeschmidt.com

Scriptures taken from the Holy Bible, New International Version®, NIV®. Copyright © 1973, 1978, 1984, 2011 by Biblica, Inc.™ Used by permission of Zondervan. All rights reserved worldwide.www.zondervan.com The "NIV" and "New International Version" are trademarks registered in the United States Patent and Trademark Office by Biblica, Inc.™

ISBN-13: 9781711700359

For every speaker, teacher and pastor who showed me how to love, respect, take comfort and find answers in the Bible.

Introduction

Did God create an evil tree?

Is there such a thing as ghosts?

Does God approve of marriages with multiple wives?

Does God not want me to marry someone of another ethnicity?

Should I cut off my hand if it sins?

Can women speak in churches?

Did Jesus go to hell?

There are many verses in the Bible that make any reader – first-timers to long-timers – go "hmmmmm." What does that mean? The statements seem contradictory or sexist or racist at first glance.

Once you understand the context and the history behind these verses, your "hmmmmm" turns into a "ahhhhhhhh!"

With over 23,000 verses in the Bible, some have to be confusing, questionable or maybe unsettling. That's okay. This is an ancient document, covering over two thousand years of history that happened over two thousand years ago.

We will always have questions, but there are always answers if we only take the time to discover them.

I hope "The 100 Most Confusing Verses in the Bible" helps you to understand those mysterious verses more clearly, not only for your own faith, but the questions that others always seem to throw at you.

Troy Schmidt
Windermere, FL
June, 2018

1. Genesis 1:4

God saw that the light was good, and he separated the light from the darkness.

So how does God separate light and darkness? What kind of a divider do you construct that puts light on this side and darkness on this side?

In Genesis 1:6-7, God divided the water in the sky from the water in the ground. The distinction here is between flowing water on and under the ground from condensation and precipitation found in the clouds. The same word used in Genesis 1:6-7 to divide the waters and is used to divide light and darkness. How did that happen?

The word for "separate" is the Hebrew word *Badal* which means "to create a distinction between." When God created the concept of light, it invaded the dark nothingness that was once there. So now light and darkness were two totally separate and opposite things. God followed up His light creation by creating things to be seen in that light – earth, water, sky, animals, birds, etc.

God created a distinction between light and darkness, a distinction that was not there before. Not everything was light and not everything was dark. So the word means "distinction" as in difference, not "separation" like some kind of mystical barrier.

2. Genesis 1:27

So God created man in his own image, in the image of God he created him; male and female he created them.

Does God look like us? This verse seems to indicate that since we have a gall bladder and an opposable thumb, that God does too. If so, does that mean God is susceptible to appendicitis and skin rashes? Does God need two eyes, one nose and two ears?

The Hebrew word for "image" is *Tselem* which means "a resemblance." We resemble God. We are a reflection of Him, not an exact replica.

Out of all the gazelles, beetles and pythons God created, only one creature closely resembles Him—man. We humans have emotional, mental and spiritual characteristics like God, such as compassion, purpose, knowledge, planning, joy, forgiveness. We get angry, hate injustice and understand right from wrong, just like our Creator.

Both males and females share those characteristics and they must come together to raise children who do the same.

The Bible says God sees with His eyes but He doesn't have retinas. The Bible says God reaches out with his arms, but He can't get bursitis. The Bible says God speaks with His mouth, but He can't bite His tongue. God does those things on a supernatural level.

So this verse is not about kneecaps, hip bones, belly buttons, heart valves and nose hairs. God created us to be like Him, not in physical ways, but in all the other ways that truly matter.

3. Genesis 2:9

The LORD God made all kinds of trees grow out of the ground—trees that were pleasing to the eye and good for food. In the middle of the garden were the tree of life and the tree of the knowledge of good and evil.

Did God create an evil tree? Was there something sinful and rotten about that tree that Adam and Eve should have run from?

The tree was not evil. The choice to eat from the tree was evil. The fruit on the tree was actually good, but deemed off limits by God, making it wrong.

It's like when a mother tells her child to not eat the yummy cookies in the jar before dinner and when the child disobeys, the child tells mom she doesn't know what's best for him.

God gave a command and for whatever reason he chose that particular tree. We must remember there were dozens of other trees to eat from, giving Adam and Eve plenty of food. This wasn't about hunger. This was about disobedience.

Evil entered through a bad choice then as it still does today. Those choices may seem good and pleasing, but that doesn't make them right.

God still has a "don't touch—don't consider—stay away from" policy with many things today. Those things aren't always evil. It's our choices that promote evil.

4. Genesis 2:22

Then the LORD **God made a woman from the rib he had taken out of the man, and he brought her to the man.**

Why did God make a woman from a man's bone? Was it to show how tough women were? And why a rib and not some other bone that doesn't taste so good with barbecue sauce on it?

The rib protects the vital organs in the body – liver, pancreas, stomach, lungs, kidneys. The rib absorbs any attack or pressure. It's a fragile bone and can break easily, but it does its job.

A woman protects a man in areas that are vital to him. As a companion, she stands by his side – where a rib is located – not behind or in front, under his foot or over his head. So of all the bones, God chose a symbolic one that represented companionship and strength.

God made man out of dust, so he can make anything out of anything. But He probably shaped woman from the DNA of the bone, so she would be similar to him – a part of him – to represent the union of the two in marriage as a symbolic reconnecting of two separate parts into one whole entity.

The two once again become one flesh when they marry.

5. Genesis 3:1

Now the serpent was more crafty than any of the wild animals the LORD God had made. He said to the woman, "Did God really say, 'You must not eat from any tree in the garden'?"

How did a snake talk and what made it more "crafty" than any other animal?

This passage is obviously not talking about a real snake. Snakes did not rebel against God. God doesn't personally hate talking snakes over all the other animals. Animals don't have freewill.

This is imagery for Satan who either took on the appearance of a snake or he was being described as "snake-like." Satan is the deceiver, tempting God's people away from following the rules.

It's unclear why Satan was never mentioned, but the imagery has always been clear. When God curses the snake in Genesis 3:14, He really curses Satan and forces him to eat dust (meaning God kicked Satan out of heaven and to the dry, dirty Earth).

In Genesis 3:15, Satan (not snakes) creates a hostility in relationships on earth and it's Satan's head who was crushed by Jesus. Jesus doesn't step on snake heads. By dying on the cross, Jesus dealt a fatal blow to Satan's progress.

Are snakes crafty, quick, able to cause problems and fear, then slip away undetected? Yes. So is Satan. The analogy works.

6. Genesis 3:7

Then the eyes of both of them were opened, and they realized they were naked; so they sewed fig leaves together and made coverings for themselves.

How were Adam and Eve's eyes opened and why did they suddenly look down and say, "Hey, we're naked"?

This verse indicates that Adam and Eve had an eye-opening experience. Nakedness as a young newlywed couple, all alone on the earth, was not big deal, now, all of a sudden it felt different.

Now they had something to hide. Now they felt vulnerable. Sin causes them to look more at themselves, their focus now on their appearance, and they felt self-conscious.

Sin makes us want to hide our inner thoughts. We fear exposure. We want to look good to the world. Sin crept into the consciousness of Adam and Eve and changed the way they saw themselves.

We do the same thing today. Fig leaves can't cover our sin. Only confession and acceptance of Jesus' death on the cross for our sins can do that.

For the first time, Adam and Eve realized their sin problem. It felt wrong. Sadly, as perpetual sinners, we've grown accustomed to that feeling. It takes the Holy Spirit working on us to feel any conviction about our sin, to look at ourselves and realize we need help.

Stop the cover-up!

7. Genesis 3:9

But the LORD God called to the man, "Where are you?"

How did God not know where Adam and Eve were? Was the garden so dense God couldn't find them?

God knew exactly where Adam and Eve were, but their actions indicated a problem. Every other time God showed up, it seems, Adam and Eve stepped out and greeted him. They walked closely together. But this time…no one welcomed Him.

So "Where are you?" is really asking "what's wrong?" and "what happened to you two?"

God wanted to know "where" they were in relationship with him. Their sin caused shame. They felt exposed (naked). They didn't want to see God face-to-face.

Their sin separated them from God. "Where are you" was a way of God asking "where are you in terms of our relationship?"

Later God asked a similar question to Cain in Genesis 4:9, "Where is your brother Abel?" He knew where Abel was, but asked the question to draw out a confession.

God still asks that question of all His people. "Where are you? Do you still love me?"

What is your answer?

8. Genesis 4:15

Then the LORD put a mark on Cain so that no one who found him would kill him.

How did God put a mark on Cain? Was Cain stamped or branded like a cow? Some have said this is when God created people of color…is that true?

The Hebrew word for *mark* is *'owth* and it has a number of meanings: a distinguishing mark, a banner, a warning, a remembrance, an omen.

Could it mean God put a distinguishing mark on Cain like changing his skin a different color? Not in the context of the passage. God "marked" Cain so one would kill him. It was a warning to people not to kill Cain for his murder—a supernatural warning label. So the mark designated Cain as special in God's eyes.

Turning Cain's skin black would not mark him as untouchable. It would mark him as different. The mark God put on him acted as an unseen protection, making sure Cain proceeded through life unmolested by the world.

In context the verse is not trying to talk about a race of people, but a special designation of Cain – a high security clearance pass that kept him safe from harm.

God showed incredible grace to the world's first murderer. He shows that grace to us today too.

9. Genesis 5:5

Altogether, Adam lived a total of 930 years, and then he died.

How did people live so long in the Bible? People today barely make it to 90.

A few factors allowed longevity in the Bible. God wanted people to live longer so they could populate the earth quickly. If people died off in their 60s, the growth of the earth would take much longer.

Also, there were not many wars because it was a tight knit family. The people were all second, third and fourth cousins, creating a tightly knit family.

A purer, freshly-created environment had less diseases and healthier foods. The air was pure and the bodies functioned to their optimum level (remember Adam's body was created to live forever so it still had the mechanics to live long).

It wasn't until Genesis 6:3 that God limited the age of people on the earth, so this incredible age spurt was not the norm. Man's predominate sinfulness caused God to step in and stop people from living so long.

10. Genesis 6:4

The Nephilim were on the earth in those days—and also afterward—when the sons of God went to the daughters of humans and had children by them. They were the heroes of old, men of renown.

Did angels have sex with humans and create a super-race of spirit humans? Who were these mysterious Nephilim?

The Hebrew *nephiyl* appears only two places in the Bible, here and Numbers 13:33. The word has always meant "giants." The Nephilim were a race of large, imposing people, like those the Israelites saw later in the Promised Land and the family of Goliath in David's time.

Were they fee-fi-fo-fum type giants? No, that's mythology and fairy tales. They were pro-wrestlers (without the steroids) or NBA centers (Shaq or Yao Ming).

The average size of a human was much smaller then, so you didn't need to be very tall to be a giant. Today people over six feet are consider tall. If you were seven foot back then you be feared! They were described here as powerful, *as if* an angel (sons of God) had a human child.

Angels don't have reproductive organs, nor can there be any other race on this earth other than what came from Adam and Eve. Don't confuse the Bible with the story of Hercules.

11. Genesis 6:6

The LORD regretted that he had made human beings on the earth, and his heart was deeply troubled.

Did God make a mistake? Did he look at humans and say, "What was I thinking?"

The word regret is *nacham* in Hebrew and it means to have sorrow. The Lord was sorry He made humans and it broke His heart.

This does not mean God made a mistake. It just means that by Genesis 6 there were few followers of God left on earth and His only option was complete destruction. Genesis 6:6 revealed that crises moment when God knew He had to send the flood.

Obviously God never gave up on humans or stopped loving them. He just needed a do-over, starting fresh with one righteous family all over again—Noah.

12. Genesis 9:24-25

When Noah awoke from his wine and found out what his youngest son had done to him, he said,

"Cursed be Canaan!
The lowest of slaves
will he be to his brothers."

Why did Noah get so mad? Did Ham do something weird to his drunk dad?

Noah, after a hard year of sailing and who knows how many years of building a cruise ship, planted a vineyard, squeezed out some grapes, allowed them to ferment, then got drunk. Passed out in his tent, Noah laid naked when his son Ham came in and saw him. So is seeing someone naked a sin?

The verse does not allude to anything inappropriate done to Noah, but speaks more to the disrespect Ham showed his dad. Ham made no attempt to cover-up Noah or sober him. He just let him lay there then went outside and told the rest of the world (which consisted of his brothers), maybe in a mocking, disrespectful tone. It's also doubtful Ham put shaving cream on Noah's hand then tickled his nose like some prankster college frat boy.

The disrespect caused Noah's outrage. The world was about to get rebooted and here was Ham laying the foundation for sin by dishonoring his mother and father. Sinfulness crept into the first family and Noah hated it.

Any hint of sinfulness could not be tolerated, explaining Noah's outrage. It's the reason the flood happened in the first place.

13. Genesis 11:9

That is why it was called Babel—because there the LORD confused the language of the whole world. From there the LORD scattered them over the face of the whole earth.

How did God confuse languages? Did He cause some to speak French, others Arabic, Turkish, Eskimo and English? Did a huge United Nations suddenly break out?

Today many languages have been influenced by other languages. English has Latin roots. Portuguese has Spanish and French influences.

God may have kickstarted a number of different tongues, but not all the languages we have today. Somehow He changed their brains, causing the parts that speak and understand to operate on a new system. Those who understood each other, gravitated toward each other and away from the others.

It was a strange and confusing moment, but it was the best way God knew how to keep the people from rebelling against Him as a whole (like they did before Noah) and causing another global annihilation.

14. Genesis 14:18

Then Melchizedek king of Salem brought out bread and wine. He was priest of God Most High...

Where did this priest come from if the temple system had not been developed? How can a man just walk out of nowhere and claim to be a priest?

The first time the word "priest" is used in the Bible is when the mysterious Melchizedek greeted Abraham with bread and wine and Abraham took up an offering to give to him. Doesn't this kind of stuff all happen later when Moses delivered the Law to the people, talking about priests and tithes?

This weird incident can be explained two ways. One, it's meant to introduce the future Israelites about what's to come in their religious system, explained thoroughly in books like Leviticus.

Two, it's meant to prophesy (or reveal) the coming Messiah. The book of Hebrews hints that Melchizedek could be Jesus himself, a king of kings and the great high priest. The town of Salem later would became Jerusalem, where the temple honored God and where Jesus died as the perfect sacrifice. Jesus served bread and wine during the Last Supper and it's to Him we give our offerings. So Abraham may have met Jesus. Pretty cool.

This strange encounter had lots of foreshadowing, made clearer as time went on.

15. Genesis 19:4-5

Before they had gone to bed, all the men from every part of the city of Sodom—both young and old—surrounded the house. They called to Lot, "Where are the men who came to you tonight? Bring them out to us so that we can have sex with them."

Was Sodom and Gomorrah destroyed because they were inhospitable to strangers? Some would like you to think that.

Middle Eastern culture demands hospitality to all and if you go there today, you will receive many invitations to come eat with them. Middle Easterners are very kind people.

However, the sin here was obvious. These strangers (angels) walked into town and were threatened with man-on-man rape. The issue was not that they did not offer appetizers to the guests and a chair to sit on, but that they wanted to commit homosexual acts on them.

Was the sin they committed the intent to rape? Yes.

Was the sin they committed homosexuality? Yes.

This wasn't about inhospitality. It was about a rampant, perverse culture that preyed on innocent people. It had gotten so bad, God needed to judge them.

16. Genesis 19:8

"Look, I have two daughters who have never slept with a man. Let me bring them out to you, and you can do what you like with them. But don't do anything to these men, for they have come under the protection of my roof."

How could Lot offer to give up his daughters to protect two strangers? Shouldn't we protect family first?

First, this offer could reflect the custom of the day where women (even your own daughters) were treated like property and guests were held higher in esteem. It seems insane and it's a good thing times have changed.

The Bible is not saying this was the right choice. It was Lot's choice and he adopted some terrible patterns of behavior living in Sodom and Gomorrah.

The other possibility could be that Lot recognized that these were angels and he did what he could to protect God's men even if it met sacrificing his daughters. Still seems crazy that he needed to step in and help two angels who were perfectly capable of protecting themselves. Again, Lot was not a righteous man.

Either way, Lot made a bad choice, never asking God what the right thing was to do. In the end, the two men, the angels, helped the family escape and the daughters made it out alive.

17. Genesis 19:26

But Lot's wife looked back, and she became a pillar of salt.

Is "looking back" a sin? Why such a terrible consequence as a result of looking over your shoulder?

Lot's wife did more than just casually glance at the incredible destruction happening behind her in Sodom and Gomorrah. She violated a direct order from an angel.

Why did the angel tell her to do this? Not only for her physical sake but for her spiritual sake. Physically her life was endangered as fireballs descended rapidly from the sky. Looking back only slowed her down.

But Lot's wife looked back and possibly mourned the end of her lifestyle, remembering fondly her days in the evil city. Life in Sodom and Gomorrah was familiar and comfortable. Sinful, sure, but Lot's family made it work, living amongst the evil and maybe even participating in it.

As a believer, we should not look back at our sinful days, thinking of them as the "good times." Maybe we had fun in college or in those early single days, but looking back too much may tempt us to recreate those moments and make those same mistakes.

For a believer, these are the good times, living in the light of God's grace with a hope and a future. And these days will only get better.

18. Genesis 19:31-32

One day the older daughter said to the younger, "Our father is old, and there is no man around here to give us children—as is the custom all over the earth. Let's get our father to drink wine and then sleep with him and preserve our family line through our father."

Why would Lot's daughters sleep with their dad (especially after he almost gave them over to a mob?)

This incident after the destruction of Sodom and Gomorrah gives us chills. Yuck. Incest.

This was not God's idea, but the daughters' idea. From their point of view, they saw no potential for reproduction amongst their people. Two major cities just got wiped out along with their husbands. Things looked desperate and they acted hastily.

God could have easily provided the right husbands to carry on their lineage, but they followed their own instincts.

In their defense, the incest rules came later in Moses' time and sleeping with relatives to keep the family fruitful was not uncommon.

However, the children born to Lot and his daughters became enemies of the Jews for years to come, proving it was not a good idea at all.

19. Genesis 20:12

"Besides, she really is my sister, the daughter of my father though not of my mother; and she became my wife."

Did Abraham marry his sister Sarah?

Yes, but technically his half sister. That doesn't make things better, but remember the incest clause in the Old Testament didn't come until the time of Moses, almost 500 years later. Sleeping with relatives was not uncommon.

In this case, unlike Lot and his daughters, God approved the union and chose Abraham and Sarah to begin a great nation.

Also, Abraham did not lie to the king of Gerar in this statement. Sarah really was his sister on a technicality. However, he did use deception to protect himself instead of relying on God for protection. God made a promise to Abraham and certainly was not going to allow him to die in the hands of King Gerar before that promise was fulfilled.

Marrying your sister is unnecessary today with a much wider population base and options for love. Besides, it's against the law.

20. Genesis 22:2

Then God said, "Take your son, your only son, whom you love—Isaac—and go to the region of Moriah. Sacrifice him there as a burnt offering on a mountain I will show you."

Does God desire child sacrifices? Absolutely not. In the Old Testament, God only asked for animal sacrifices.

So why did He ask Abraham to take his one and only son to the mountain and sacrifice him?

God had no intention to see the sacrifice continue. He only wanted to see if Abraham could surrender the most important thing in his life. Was he willing to "bring the knife down" putting his love for God before everything else?

We can say we are willing to give up things for God, but are we ready to light the match to burn it up, pick it up to throw it overboard, hit the switch and blow it up? Do we have the willingness to sacrifice the most important things in our life to God?

Abraham passed the test and revealed his faith in God. Over a thousand years later, God sacrificed His own son on this same mountain showing Abraham's descendants that He was willing to follow through to show His love for sinners.

What are you willing to bring the knife down and surrender to God?

21. Genesis 25:34

So Esau despised his birthright.

How can you hate your birthright? Is it like hating your birthday? What difference did it make that Esau gave it up to his brother Jacob?

Birthright meant inheritance and legacy. The firstborn got all the privileges, power and a higher percentage of the profits. The firstborn position in the family came with responsibility.

Esau's rejection of that birthright meant he devalued his family and could care less about his legacy. He wanted no part of it. He rejected the responsibility. Esau saw no worth in his future. It was all about what he wanted now. A cup of stew sounded better.

Jacob wanted the birthright position and had the cunning to make it work. He proved to be the better firstborn. Esau's rejection buried his family legacy into obscurity. Jacob's effort produced a family line with Jesus Christ.

We shouldn't despise where we were born in our family. We were born right where we needed to be, at the time and place God destined us to enter into this family. God will use us to bring Jesus Christ to the world in our own unique way.

22. Genesis 26:8-9

When Isaac had been there a long time, Abimelek king of the Philistines looked down from a window and saw Isaac caressing his wife Rebekah. So Abimelek summoned Isaac and said, "She is really your wife! Why did you say, 'She is my sister'?"

Wait, is this déjà vu? Didn't Isaac's father Abraham do the same thing?

Yes, actually this happened three times in Genesis. Abraham tricked Pharaoh in Genesis 12 into thinking Sarah was his sister and then again Abraham said the same thing to Abimelek, king of Gerar in Genesis 20.

Then Isaac found himself in a similar situation as his father and used the same deception with a king by the same name - Abimelek king of the Philistines in Gerar. Was it the same person? Hard to say. Could be or maybe Abimelek Jr.

This Abimelek was not fooled as quickly, so he definitely learned from the first encounter.

The point of this repeated action focused more on Isaac acting without faith like his father Abraham and turning to deception, instead of trusting God to take care of his family.

We must be careful or our children will commit the same mistakes as us.

23. Genesis 29:28

And Jacob did so. He finished the week with Leah, and then Laban gave him his daughter Rachel to be his wife.

Situations like this in Genesis make one think that God believes in polygamy. Absolutely not.

Adam, Noah and Isaac were monogamous. Abraham used Hagar as a child producer or surrogate (wrongfully), but did not marry her. Abraham technically had one wife, Sarah.

In this situation, Jacob was tricked. He wanted one wife, Rachel, and woke up with her sister, Leah, after making love to her in the dark after a huge party. Now that she was defiled, Jacob did the right thing and kept her, but still wanted to stick to the original plan. So he married Rachel too.

None of this was God's plan. All of it was man's plan.

God used Jacob's relationship status – made more complicated by two more concubines – to make twelve tribes, but, remember, all of that operated outside God's original intention for marriage…one man and one woman.

While the Bible communicates polygamy during that time, God never endorsed it.

24. Genesis 32:28

Then the man said, "Your name will no longer be Jacob, but Israel, because you have struggled with God and with humans and have overcome."

Jacob in Genesis 32 wrestled with a man, who was an angel. So how did Jacob really wrestle with God? And how does one even declare a draw after such an encounter?

Jacob goes mano-y-mano with this angel in the wilderness after leaving his father-in-law Laban. The encounter served as a symbolic gesture of his own struggle with God.

The "man" Jacob wrestled with finished the match by renaming Jacob "The Struggler." The name fit. Jacob consistently turned to his own deceptions in order to make things work, in terms of his birthright and his job. Finally, at this stage in his life, Jacob began to turn his focus to his relationship with God. But it was a struggle.

Jacob wrestled a flesh and blood man, but it was an angel in physical form, a representative of God, standing in for God. The angel could have killed Jacob, but allowed him to live as a reminder that you can't struggle with God for too long without getting hurt (the angel sprained Jacob's hip, causing permanent damage).

While Jacob physically struggled with an angel, he spiritually struggled with God.

25. Genesis 38:9-10

But Onan knew that the child would not be his; so whenever he slept with his brother's wife, he spilled his semen on the ground to keep from providing offspring for his brother. What he did was wicked in the LORD's sight; so the LORD put him to death also.

Is this verse saying masturbation is a sin?

Onan's sin was a refusal to do the right thing and marrying his sister in law after his brother's death. This practice kept the family's property secure and made sure outsiders did not infiltrate the family's inheritance. Plus a previously married woman was not preferred over a virgin, so she would have had a hard time moving on in life.

Onan didn't want to do the honorable thing and refused to impregnate his sister in law. His anger and hatred for his family line infuriated God.

So this was not a masturbation issue. This was an obedience issue.

This is not to say masturbation is okay. Masturbation coincides with lust and self-pleasure and would be regarded a sin for those reasons, but this verse would not directly support that idea.

26. Genesis 42:8

Although Joseph recognized his brothers, they did not recognize him.

How could Joseph's brothers not recognize him? A few reasons...

First of all, they thought he was dead or at least a slave. Who could imagine he would the Chief of Staff for Pharaoh?

Joseph spoke Egyptian. Their brother never did that.

Joseph, as a leader, probably kept his distance from the people. It's not like the Oval Office and a President slapping your back and shaking your hand.

Joseph may have taken on the grooming trends of the culture. Egyptians were clean shaven, so maybe he didn't look like himself.

Joseph was a boy when he left them and years later was now a man. He passed through adolescence into adulthood. Years in a prison and now in a palace physically changed him.

Finally, maybe God just kept the brothers from realizing Joseph's identity. The final revelation was a great moment in Genesis and a real tide-turner.

27. Exodus 7:3-4

But I will harden Pharaoh's heart, and though I multiply my signs and wonders in Egypt, he will not listen to you.

If God hardens hearts, what happened to freewill and was it fair that Pharaoh seemingly had no chance to repent?

God does not mess with freewill, but He messes with the intensity of that freewill. Pharaoh was not a believer in a God. He believed in himself. Pharaoh never would have accepted God, though he had moments of confession. That confession was superficial, only to serve Pharaoh's needs.

God exploited that hard heart and made it harder. Why? To make the story of Exodus better. So God would get more glory. Pharaoh appeared weak and asked for prayer, but he did so only to take the pain away, not to gain a Savior.

By Pharaoh's choice, Pharaoh never had a chance to believe. But God could use Pharaoh's hard heart to break through other hard hearts who softened when they saw God's power displayed in Exodus.

28. Exodus 20:7

"You shall not misuse the name of the LORD your God, for the LORD will not hold anyone guiltless who misuses his name."

What does it mean to "misuse" or to use God's name in vain?

The Hebrew word for *misuse* is *shav'* and it means "emptiness" or "worthlessness."

This commandment includes using God's name in a curse, but it also means using God's name casually too. If I say God's name as an exclamation or shock, I could be calling out to Him, but if I'm not, I've reduced his name to nothing more than the phrase "Oh wow." Worthless.

I could also misuse God's name in a joke or speak for Him. Anytime I use God's name for anything other than praise or prayer or educational purposes, I could be guilty of breaking this commandment.

So use God's name sparingly and purposefully. Make sure when you use God's name, it has meaning and glory.

29. Exodus 33:20

But," he said, "you cannot see my face, for no one may see me and live."

Didn't Moses see God and live? Didn't the Bible say Moses saw God face-to-face?

Not entirely. God told Moses that he could only see His back, like a trail to a comet. Moses witnessed God's departing presence, a glimpse of him passing.

Why would seeing the face of God kill you?

The face of God would be the face of ultimate holiness and righteousness. It would cause such fear in your heart and stop it from beating. His holiness would be so shocking to our sinfulness that our bodies could not see any reason to live. Everything we propped up our lives with would collapse when we stared truth in the eyes. Our earthly life becomes meaningless.

We can only see God when we die, when our earthly heart has stopped beating and our spiritual heart takes over completely. Then we enter eternity gazing at God's holiness and righteousness, unable to die from the shock, but existing eternally in awe.

30. Exodus 34:14

Do not worship any other god, for the LORD, whose name is Jealous, is a jealous God.

Isn't jealousy a bad thing? How can God be jealous and it be a good thing but if I'm jealous it's a bad thing?

The word used for "jealous" is *qanna* and it's only used for God in terms of rivals. For man the word for *jealous* is *qin'ah* and it means a sexual passion.

God hates those rivals battling for our spiritual attention. He can't stand the other gods that we set up for ourselves and worship over Him.

For humans, we experience the same kind of jealousy when something rivals our love for our children and it pulls them away from us. That is a good jealousy.

The bad jealousy is the kind that is a sexual passion, when we only want someone for sex and deny that they can have a relationship with someone else. A jealous person doesn't care for the other person's heart, only their own body.

It's a good thing God is jealous for us. It shows the passion He has for an exclusive relationship with us.

31. Leviticus 4:2

"Say to the Israelites: 'When anyone sins unintentionally and does what is forbidden in any of the LORD's commands...'"

How can you sin unintentionally?

Intentional sin occurs when you enter into a situation ready to sin and knowingly do the wrong thing. Call it malice forethought.

Unintentional sin happens by accident. It could cover everything from clicking on a link that takes you to a picture of a naked person and having a lustful thought, to negligence by waving around a stick in someone's face and poking out their eye, to outright stupidity by driving your car down the road without any hands and crashing into a fruit stand.

Ignorance is not an alibi. No police officer lets you get by saying, "I didn't know there was a law against that" or "I didn't know what the speed limit was."

We make a mistake not wanting to make a mistake, but doing accidentally things that can lead to a mistake. That's unintentional.

So we need to pray, "God help me to not sin unintentionally" as much as we ask God to deliver us from intentional sin. Both can be harmful to our lives.

32. Leviticus 11:10

But all creatures in the seas or streams that do not have fins and scales—whether among all the swarming things or among all the other living creatures in the water—you are to regard as unclean.

Is eating shrimp a sin? It was. Lobster too.

The Old Testament dietary laws emphasized clean foods to create a clean lifestyle and mindset in the Jews. As they made clean choices, they understood why they should be free of sin.

Many of those animals listed lived in the dirty poop of the creatures swimming above them or consumed the carcasses of dead animals. Sound delicious? God protected His people from the possibility of contamination, giving them healthy dietary choices.

But those restrictions need not apply any longer. Peter's Acts 10 dream of unclean animals revealed to a New Testament audience that the dietary laws no longer applied. The law was no longer about keeping yourself free of sin, but God's grace through Jesus Christ now kept us free of sin.

Jesus died for all sins and now makes us sin-free. We no longer need to look at our plate as a reminder, but to the cross.

Enjoy all the shrimp and lobster you want, but maybe you still want to stay away from the broiled vulture.

33. Leviticus 19:19

Do not mate different kinds of animals.

Do not plant your field with two kinds of seed.

Do not wear clothing woven of two kinds of material.

Why does God care about mixing animals, seeds and clothes?

Our God is not concerned about creating mutant, cross-species animals like the jack-a-lope (jack rabbit and antelope). He isn't worried about mixing peas with tomatoes and creating pea-matoes. God isn't trying to qualify as a guest judge on Project Runway, furious at the mixing of polyesters and cottons.

God wanted the Israelites' daily lives to be reminded of separation. As they separated themselves from the outside world – those who worshipped other gods – they needed to remember that principle when they worked with livestock, planted their fields, even when they got dressed in the morning.

Today our reminder of separation comes from Jesus Christ, who called us to go out into the world, but not to be "of" the world.

Jesus mixed with society but didn't get mixed-up by it.

34. Leviticus 24:14

"Take the blasphemer outside the camp. All those who heard him are to lay their hands on his head, and the entire assembly is to stone him."

Why aren't we stoning blasphemers and adulterers today?

Punishments like this were reserved for the newly formed state of Israel. Exodus and Leviticus (Deuteronomy too) outlined the laws for God's nation. The rules clearly stated that no sin would be tolerated in that community. Israel would be the model for a sinless society that did not allow worldly practices into their nation.

The punishment for sin was death. The society would not tolerate sin just like God does not tolerate sin. There was no court system and lawyers so the responsibility rested on the community to bring justice.

Things are different today, but the punishment for sin is still death—not by the judicial system, but by the heavenly system. However, we have a savior, Jesus Christ, who took on that punishment for us. He took on the pain, bled and was buried for us.

However, Jesus rolled away the stone so we would not have to be stoned for our sins.

35. Leviticus 26:18

"If after all this you will not listen to me, I will punish you for your sins seven times over."

God seems like He needs anger management at times.

Punishing people seven times over seems excessive. One punishment from God is enough. But seven? Why does God seem so angry?

In Leviticus, God was establishing a nation that represented His character and followed His rules. A great plan, until sinful people stood in His way.

As Moses led the Israelites through the wilderness, people like Achan, Korah, Dathan, Abiram all led groups like the Rowdy Rebellion Club and the Sabbath Breakers Society. If God let their actions slide without repercussions, others would use God's leniency as their excuse to break more rules.

So God had to punish harshly and thoroughly to remind others of the consequences of sin. He wanted to create a positive fear in His children for their own good.

Excessive? Maybe, until you understand that wages of sin is death. God was saving many by punishing a few.

36. Numbers 22:28

Then the LORD opened the donkey's mouth, and it said to Balaam, "What have I done to you to make you beat me these three times?" So donkeys can talk in the Bible?

Well, not all donkeys, just this one. The prophet Balaam stubbornly moved ahead of God and to get Balaam's attention God allowed the donkey to speak. God wanted to show this prophet that a dumb ol' donkey had more sense than a wise ol' prophet.

How did the donkey talk? Did it grow vocal chords? Do all animals have the capability to speak but we don't understand them? Is the story of Dr. Doolittle true?

Look, God can do anything. If He wants to make a donkey talk, then a donkey could talk. Or what could have happened was something more along the lines of a ventriloquist. God moved the donkey's lips but the words came from Him (or an angel).

Either way, the point impacted Balaam who saw the error of his ways through a miraculous talking donkey.

Thankfully animals don't talk, but if they do, you should probably pay attention to what they have to say (or seek professional attention).

37. Numbers 23:19

"God is not human, that he should lie, not a human being, that he should change his mind. Does he speak and then not act? Does he promise and not fulfill?"

Does God change his mind? Didn't God change his mind with Moses?

Then the Lord relented and did not bring on his people the disaster he had threatened. Exodus 32:19

If a man changes his mind, it means he received new information that he did not expect and alters his line of thinking based on new evidence.

God can make a stand then change that stand when the circumstances change, but that doesn't mean He changed his mind. God can change His tactic or back off on His strategy, but He knew all the options that would occur. In the case of Moses, God made a stance then waited for Moses to humbly plead for mercy. The purpose was to get Moses to step in the gap for the people. Once He accomplished His purpose, God backed off on His threat.

God relents when He sees our repentance. It's what He was striving for in the first place.

38. Deuteronomy 5:9

You shall not bow down to them or worship them; for I, the Lord your God, am a jealous God, punishing the children for the sin of the parents to the third and fourth generation of those who hate me... Does God punish the children for the sins their parents committed?

The Bible seems to contradict itself especially in verses like this:

Fathers shall not be put to death for their children, nor children put to death for their fathers; each is to die for his own sin. **Deuteronomy 24:16**

These verses say two different things. Deuteronomy 5 talks about punishment. Deuteronomy 24 talks about death. Children will not be put to death for the sin of their parents, but they will receive a punishment for the parents' sin. What is that punishment? Consequences. An alcoholic father passes alcoholic tendencies on to his children. An abusive mother teaches abuse to her children.

Ezekiel 18 says both parent and child will die because they sin. In other words, everyone is directly responsible for their actions. There are no excuses—blaming your parents for the way you were raised doesn't hold up in court.

The punishment of consequences can be passed on to future generations and yet they don't have to. You can stop the cycle by stopping the sin through your own freewill.

39. Deuteronomy 7:3

Do not intermarry with them. Do not give your daughters to their sons or take their daughters for your sons...

When God tells people not to intermarry, doesn't He sound like a racist?

Intermarriage in the Old Testimony had more to do with mixing cultures than races. The culture of every other nation in the Bible focused on worshipping other gods and those people brought their gods into those relationships. God didn't want His people tempted by those gods.

Moses had an inter-national marriage with Zipporah, who was a Cushite woman (which could be Egyptian, Ethiopian or African) and their relationship caused some controversy (Numbers 12:1) mostly because of jealousy by Moses' siblings.

God does not frown on interracial marriages. He does not want a Christian marrying a non-Christian which could cause the believer to be drawn away from him. That's the only intermarriage a believer should avoid today.

40. Deuteronomy 22:5

A woman must not wear men's clothing, nor a man wear women's clothing, for the LORD your God detests anyone who does this.

Is Tyler Perry a sinner dressing up like Madea?

The purpose behind this law was to deter gender bending. Men needed to be men as they were created to be and women needed to act like women as they were created to be.

The motivation behind this cross-dressing was also called into question. Was the person trying to entice others of the same gender to have sex? Could a guy mislead another guy into having sex with him by pretending to be a woman?

Also, cross-dressing was probably part of some religious practices that worshipped gods who promoted sex.

So all of these factors – design, deception, temptation and the abomination of worshipping other gods – led to this commandment against cross-dressing.

Cross-dressing for laughs isn't necessarily a sin but it begins to blur the lines that can eventually lead to the acceptance of it later on.

41. Joshua 6:21

They devoted the city to the LORD and destroyed with the sword every living thing in it—men and women, young and old, cattle, sheep and donkeys.

Why would God ask for women and children to be killed (donkeys too)?

The creation of the nation of Israel was a unique task for God. The only time in history He ever attempted it. So He required high standards of Israel that He didn't require of other nations at war during any other time.

Israel was to reflect the nature of God by being clean of all sin. They were to reflect God in everything they did and take steps to confess and remove their sin.

To do that, they could not interact with outsiders who did not desire to be followers of God. So the Israel army did not come to convert, but to remove those enemies from the land as judgment for the sins that nation had done. The enemy women and children still living post-war would only stir up dissension during their lifetimes. The donkeys and sheep were killed to show that the nation was not attacked for their resources, but destroyed because of the nation's sin.

God does not remove some sin from our lives. He removes all sin from our lives. If there's a hint of sin left in us, it will always spring up and infect the rest of us. That theme was brutally carried out when the Israelites took over a city.

The goal of the Israelite army was separation and complete annihilation of all that was unholy. It's not God's design for wars today.

42. Judges 6:39

Then Gideon said to God, "Do not be angry with me. Let me make just one more request. Allow me one more test with the fleece, but this time make the fleece dry and let the ground be covered with dew."

Isn't it a sin to test God? When Gideon tested God by asking him to make the fleece wet with dew one morning while the ground was dry and then switching it by asking God to make the fleece dry and the ground wet…wasn't Gideon testing God?

Testing God in the Bible was more like what the Pharisees did to Jesus – questioning him with tough questions and asking Him to do incredible tasks with the motive to disprove him and make him look irrelevant.

Gideon sought confirmation of God's will since God asked him to go to war against the idolatry in Israel and fight the scary Midianite enemy. It was a huge ask and Gideon could have died. Many people's lives were on the line. Gideon moved slowly, carefully and thoughtfully.

God is happy to confirm his purpose and existence if you just ask. It's not a test if you want to know the answers.

43. Judges 11:39

After the two months, she returned to her father, and he did to her as he had vowed. And she was a virgin.

Did God accept a child sacrifice from Jephthah?

In this passage, Jepthah made a rash vow when he asked God to deliver his enemies into his hands. He promised to sacrifice the first thing that came through his door when he got home after victory. Jepthah hoped a goat would walk out when he arrived. Instead, his daughter ran out. Uh-oh.

Jepthah didn't need to make that vow. God only wanted him to defeat the enemies. No vow was needed to prove one's worthiness. Only God's promise was required.

Jepthah felt he had to follow through with his vow but it was his daughter who allowed the vow to be satisfied. The one who would be killed offered to be the sacrifice.

God didn't ask for it. The daughter did.

In the same way, Jesus allowed Himself to die as a sacrifice for our mistakes. God asked for it. Jesus confirmed it.

While it was a truly heroic and honorable deed the daughter did, it did not show that God asked for human sacrifices.

44. Judges 16:19

After putting him to sleep on her lap, she called for someone to shave off the seven braids of his hair, and so began to subdue him. And his strength left him.

Was Samson's strength in his hair?

It certainly seemed that way since once his hair was cut, he lost his strength.

Actually, Samson's strength was in Samson's vow to be a Nazirite. A Nazirite vowed to do three things: not consume wine or fermented drink, stay away from dead things and not cut one's hair. In Samson's life he drank wine, touched dead bodies (animals and people) and then eventually broke his last promise when he gave away the secret of his strength – cutting his hair.

His hair represented his promise to be God's man. His sin caused that vow to be broken, so God removed all his strength.

Later, in prison, Samson's hair grew back and so did his commitment to God. He left the earth tearing down the temple and taking many Philistines with him.

Our strength is not in our hair. Our strength is found in keeping our promises to God.

45. 1 Samuel 28:13-14

The king said to her, "Don't be afraid. What do you see?"

The woman said, "I see a ghostly figure coming up out of the earth."

"What does he look like?" he asked.

"An old man wearing a robe is coming up," she said.

Then Saul knew it was Samuel, and he bowed down and prostrated himself with his face to the ground.

When Samuel called up the spirit of Samuel, using a medium, to ask him some questions, Samuel's spirit came to life and spoke to Samuel.

Was that a ghost? Well, not in the Halloween sense of spirits walking around at night, scaring people and causing mischief. Spirits do not run around and do whatever they want.

When we die, our spirits go to one of two places with no interaction in the physical world. They are locked in and securely in place until the resurrection.

In Samuel's case, God allowed his spirit to come forth only for this one purpose. It was a judgment on Saul for trying to consult mediums and spirits. Even the medium was shocked because this kind of thing never happened before.

This is not a world we should mess with. Don't try to talk to dead people. Talk to God for comfort and direction.

46. 2 Samuel 1:15

Then David called one of his men and said, "Go, strike him down!" So he struck him down, and he died.

A man came to David and said he had killed King Saul, the crazed king who pursued David so viciously. David responded and ordered that the man be killed for killing King Saul. Isn't that an odd request? Wasn't King Saul trying to kill David? Didn't the man do David a favor?

It is unless you know David. David had opportunities to kill Saul and refused. David stayed loyal to his king even though the king tried to kill David. David had a heart like no other and his loyalty must be commended.

There is some discrepancy in the man's story, too. 1 Samuel 30:4 says Saul fell on his sword. The man showed up and said he killed Saul. Maybe David sensed the man was seeking a reward or glory for killing Saul.

In that case, David's order to kill the man made perfect sense for this reward-seeker. He was punished for lying to the king.

47. 2 Samuel 2:2

So David went up there with his two wives, Ahinoam of Jezreel and Abigail, the widow of Nabal of Carmel.

Does God encourage polygamy?

David was described as a man after God's own heart. Was marrying multiple wives part of the heart of God?

While the characters of the Bible took multiple wives, God never directed them to do so.

Every time a man took two or more wives, problems occurred, especially in David's case.

David's half-children quarreled and jockeyed for power. There was little unity amongst them.

The Genesis account of God bringing Eve to Adam remains the standard to this day. It's the perfect union of one man and one woman that God desires and it'll never work any other way.

48. 2 Samuel 10:4

So Hanun seized David's envoys, shaved off half of each man's beard, cut off their garments at the buttocks, and sent them away.

What kind of punishment is shaving a beard down the middle and making the victim run around half-naked with their butts showing? Sounds more like a fraternity stunt. And why would it instigate an act of war against the Ammonites?

Would you want to walk around your city looking like this? Didn't think so. You would look crazy. People would smirk and raise an eyebrow. It didn't feel very good for these men either.

While it seems funny, this humiliation happened to political envoys. Imagine if our ambassador and his staff went to a funeral of a nation's president and they were stripped naked and pelted with whipped cream pies, all of it put on YouTube for all the world to see. We would be outraged.

Through this act, Hanun told David to "butt out" of their business (sorry) or face more humiliation. David's army, led by Joab, spanked the Ammonites (couldn't resist) for treating their act of kindness so rudely.

49. 2 Samuel 24:13

So Gad went to David and said to him, "Shall there come on you three years of famine in your land? Or three months of fleeing from your enemies while they pursue you? Or three days of plague in your land? Now then, think it over and decide how I should answer the one who sent me."

Why would God punish the people for David's sin? All this torture for David taking a census? Seems harsh.

A leader's sin has consequences on his people. From presidents to pastors, what happens in private has very public ramifications.

By sinning, David jeopardized God's relationship with his nation. David must live as the example God intended Israel to represent. By taking a census, David trusted more in the numbers of his army than the strength of God. So God punished the people David trusted in to show David He could take away the numbers. "Now, who do you trust more, David?"

God showed grace when He backed off on the punishment and didn't fully carry it out once His point was made.

It's hard for a selfish leader to see others get hurt by what they did. However, true repentance can only occur when a leader faces great sorrow. God taught David and the nation a lesson in trust.

50. 1 Kings 11:3

He had seven hundred wives of royal birth and three hundred concubines, and his wives led him astray.

How could a wise king have 700 wives?

Solomon asked for wisdom from God and got it, but that doesn't mean God's wisdom automatically took over Solomon's freewill. Solomon needed to still choose the wisdom, yet he chose selfish endeavors.

700 wives is a little over the top. Just a touch.

Solomon thought he was being smart marrying the daughters of kings in the surrounding area. His efforts brought the greatest time of peace to Israel. While the nations were not at war, battles were brewing inside his borders. These women brought foreign gods to Israel, which Solomon acknowledged and permitted. One generation later, his oldest son Rehoboam saw his dad's recklessness and chose unwisely, causing the nation to split.

Solomon had access to more wisdom than anyone ever did. However, he allowed excess to dominate his kingdom, from the building programs to the relationships he established.

51. Job 1:8

Then the LORD said to Satan, "Have you considered my servant Job? There is no one on earth like him; he is blameless and upright, a man who fears God and shuns evil."

Why would God bring up someone's name to Satan?

Most of us would be like, "Hey God, keep my name on the down low when talking to Satan. I don't want him to get any ideas."

God knew what he was doing even though the suggestion disrupted Job's life and many died. Why? God wanted to show Satan that there were still righteous people on this earth. That no matter how horribly Satan treated humans, the good ones still come out of it loving God.

This story has certainly helped many lives as we all marvel at Job's character through suffering. The story of Job has kept many from cursing God during their own struggles and seeing the purpose of suffering.

If your story had the power to affect millions of lives, wouldn't you find all your suffering and turmoil worthwhile?

The story of Job shows us that God protects us through it all and He wants our testimonies to give hope to others.

52. Psalm 61:4

I long to dwell in your tent forever and take refuge in the shelter of your wings.

Does God have wings? Is He like an angel?

God doesn't have wings. Only feathery birds and angels have wings (six of them actually).

Psalms uses metaphors and in this passage the writer wanted to communicate the protective nature of God by comparing him to a bird that puts her young on a wing.

For a baby bird, that is a safe, warm and comforting place to be.

In other Psalms, the writers describe God as a shelter, a rock or a wall. Not very soft and fuzzy.

We can't always get literal interpretations from Psalms, but we can get a deeper, expressive meaning from the poetic language in Psalms.

53. Psalm 98:8

**Let the rivers clap their hands,
let the mountains sing together for joy;**

How do rivers clap? How do mountains sing?

They don't, but if they could, they would.

Jesus even said stones would cry out to praise Him. Maybe singing a little rock 'n roll?

Creation knows who deserves all the praise yet they don't have mouths to express it. So how does creation express its praise?

The psalmist poetically sees the waves clapping on to the shoreline as praise.

He sees the wind singing through the mountains as praise.

By just doing what it was made to do, the creation praises God.

We can praise God too but just doing what we were made to do.

54. Proverbs 25:21-22

If your enemy is hungry, give him food to eat; if he is thirsty, give him water to drink. In doing this, you will heap burning coals on his head, and the LORD will reward you.

Why would putting burning coals on someone's head be a good thing? Won't that make them "hot-headed"?

In context, this is referenced as a good thing. By providing for someone in need, you "heap the burning coals on their head."

One idea stems from a practice of providing someone coals if their fire went out. They would carry the hot coals in a container on their head to their home. This would provide them with heat and warmth.

The second idea focuses on purification. A hot coal cauterizes an infected wound, removing the bacteria. By being kind to others, you cauterize the hate in their mind (head) and allow them to be more forgiving and loving.

So don't literally throw hot coals at your neighbor. Instead, pour on the love and burn away the hate.

55. Ecclesiastes 1:2

"Meaningless! Meaningless!"
    says the Teacher.
"Utterly meaningless!
    Everything is meaningless."

What's a verse like this doing in the Bible? Meaningless? How can this be a lesson to learn from God's word?

King Solomon had a life of excess – all the wisdom, women, wine and wealth he wanted. When God asked Solomon what he wanted most of all, Solomon asked for wisdom to lead the people. God granted him that wish and gave him all the things he didn't ask for, like wealth and power.

Solomon ruled during the most peaceful era in Israel's history. However, peace makes people soft and their faith weakens. Solomon stupidly made mistakes, grabbing all the excess he could find.

Toward the end of his life Solomon summed up what it was like to have everything you could ever want on this earth – meaningless.

Solomon did not say life was meaningless, but a life that pursues comfort, power, riches and treasures was meaningless. That's the message of the Bible.

Seek the unseen and reject the power of the seen. You'll find meaning in God and meaningless in the world.

56. Ecclesiastes 7:3

**Frustration is better than laughter,
because a sad face is good for the heart.**

This seems more like the motto of the Pessimists Society than a verse in the Bible. Why would Solomon be a Debbie Downer?

If Paul had access to emojis, he certainly would have put one at the end of this sentence. ☹

In Ecclesiastes 7, Solomon contrasted the carefree lifestyle of a fool with the hard life of a person facing difficulties. The fool ignores his problems and parties like there is no tomorrow. A wise person faces the issues today and deals with them. His heart is strengthened as he grows in faith.

Both of them have problems but the wise person at least recognizes them and deals with them. Yes it causes his life to be frustrated and sad, but at least he's not lost in some fantasy world where problems don't exist.

He's being real, not fake.

So don't feel bad if life's got you down. At least you're not ignoring the problem. Face your problem with faith and turn that frown upside down.

57. Ecclesiastes 10:19

**A feast is made for laughter,
wine makes life merry,
and money is the answer for everything.**

So is money the answer for everything?

Once again, like other verses in Ecclesiastes, out of context it appears Solomon supports the notion that money can buy you happiness.

But look at the other two lines of this verse. People have parties with the sole purpose of laughing. They drink wine to get all crazy. Those kind of people think money solves all their problems.

Solomon addressed the party people who think a huge blow-out, filled with gluttony and drunkenness, will make life better. They believe their idea of throwing money at things is the easiest and best solution.

Solomon actually disagrees with this sentiment after making his point for eleven chapters.

By chapter 12 he gives the only answer to life's pursuit of wealth and power – Remember the God of your youth.

Everything other than God is meaningless.

58. Song of Songs 4:2

**Your teeth are like a flock of sheep just shorn,
  coming up from the washing.
Each has its twin;
  not one of them is alone.**

Your teeth are like a flock of sheep? What? Obviously this guy didn't write for Hallmark.

Some of the "pick-up" lines in Song of Songs fall short to our high standards of "Roses are red, violets are blue."

Solomon looked for a comparison of his bride's white teeth and with few choices to choose from – plants, animals and nature – he mentions the whitest thing she could identify with: Freshly sheared (all the dirt and burrs removed) and recently washed sheep.

By calling them "twins" he's really saying her teeth are matched, not uneven or even missing. Every tooth has a companion tooth. She's got a full set of teeth, which would be a blessing in the days before dentists and fluoride toothpaste.

Solomon does a great job in Song of Songs of being specific about what he finds beautiful about his bride. Never just tell a woman "You look good." Be specific – "I like that color dress on you" or "Those earrings match your eyes."

And if you're feeling brave tell her, "I like that you have all your teeth and they're not stained either." Try it.

59. Isaiah 64:6

All of us have become like one who is unclean, and all our righteous acts are like filthy rags; we all shrivel up like a leaf, and like the wind our sins sweep us away.

Is doing a nice thing for others really that bad? This verse makes it sound like our good deeds have no more value than a filthy rag.

This verse isn't saying helping old ladies across the street or cutting your neighbor's lawn are despicable acts. This verse is saying that those actions in the eyes of God don't wipe away our sins.

A filthy rag cannot pick up dirt because it's filled with dirt. It will smear the mess, making a greater mess. So a sinful life that tries to do righteous deeds cannot make anything cleaner.

Also, we cannot do enough righteous deeds to clean up the mess our sin caused. It would be like trying to clean up an oil tanker spill with a handkerchief.

So the rag needs to be clean first, washed as white as snow. God cleans us up by forgiving our sins through Jesus Christ. Only then can we be used to do righteous acts for God.

Ask God to clean up your heart, then you can clean up your act.

60. Jeremiah 13:4

"Take the belt you bought and are wearing around your waist, and go now to Perath and hide it there in a crevice in the rocks."

What does God have against belts? Nothing. God likes belts. They keep our pants up. If those pants drop, we would be ashamed. God doesn't want us to be ashamed of our sins and so in this case, belts signify obedience.

God asked Jeremiah to wear a linen belt then hide it in the rocks. Days later he went to dig the belt up and found it ruined and useless.

That belt symbolized Judah and Jerusalem and their great pride. Over time, as they tried to hide from God and isolate themselves, they too would become ruined.

God asked the prophet Jeremiah to do many physical actions to reveal a spiritual purpose. God used these examples to teach His people about obedience.

Sadly the people did not listen to Jeremiah and their sin caused them great shame.

61. Jeremiah 31:29

"In those days people will no longer say,

'The parents have eaten sour grapes,
   and the children's teeth are set on edge.'"

Is this a prophecy for dentists? Were grapes the candy of the Old Testament times?

While dental hygiene could be passed on genetically, it could also be passed on relationally as the children watch their parents forget to floss, consume candy and balk at brushing.

This common saying during the days of Jeremiah (and Ezekiel) talked about passing down a legacy of sin. It expressed the thought that a parent's sin was passed on to future generations.

While it's true that a parent's sin has consequences that affect future generations – alcoholism, adultery, abuse – it doesn't mean that it's automatically an issue. Many children work through the issues and come out better.

It also doesn't mean that God judges a future generation for the sin of a past generation. However, if the current generation adopts the same sin and commits it too, they will face the same judgment.

Be a role model to your kids in the way you treat others (and maybe even in the way your treat your teeth).

62. Ezekiel 1:10

Their faces looked like this: Each of the four had the face of a human being, and on the right side each had the face of a lion, and on the left the face of an ox; each also had the face of an eagle.

Ezekiel did drugs, right? These kind of visions seem more like hallucinations caused by bad mushrooms. If these creatures are from God, why are they so weird?

Ezekiel, as well as prophets like David and John, saw some crazy stuff. They tried to convey their wild visions into the limitations of a few words.

Here Ezekiel described what the vision looked *like*. The creature (in this case an angel) had a four-sided face that had the appearance of a human, a lion, an ox and an eagle. That's the best way he could describe it.

Maybe the vision meant to convey clues that Ezekiel and others were to discover over time. These four animals appear in other visions in other scripture and were meant to be cross-referenced (like later in Revelation). The four descriptions reveal characteristics about the angels (a body shape like humans, the courage of lions, the strength of an ox, the wings of eagles). Trying to describe the supernatural world using common, natural language would look weird in our world, but perfectly natural in the next.

The vision was meant to disturb Ezekiel and his fellow Israelites and cause them to pay attention. It still gets our attention today. There are things in the supernatural world that we can't explain or describe accurately in this world.

63. Ezekiel 1:16

This was the appearance and structure of the wheels: They sparkled like topaz, and all four looked alike. Each appeared to be made like a wheel intersecting a wheel.

Did Ezekiel see a flying saucer? A cylindrical flying object with sparkling lights?

First of all there is no such thing as flying saucers and space aliens from another planet. We should be able to just end the discussion there.

So what was this that Ezekiel saw? In his vision, the wheels wrapped around the four living creatures which were angels. The wheels could have represented three things:

1. The energy created by the presence of these four angels. Hold two hot wires together and sparks fly. Maybe the same thing happens when four angels decide to hang out.
2. The workings of the angels are like gears. When wheels turn, work is being done, whether it represents gears in a factory or wheels on a truck. When these four angels get together, work is being done.
3. A dazzling light show to get Ezekiel's attention. Look at the pretty lights, Ezekiel! Isn't God spectacular!

Remember this is a vision so interpretations run rampant. It meant something to Ezekiel and got his attention at the beginning of the vision so he would respond to the rest of the words passed on to him forty chapters later.

64. Ezekiel 4:12

"Eat the food as you would a loaf of barley bread; bake it in the sight of the people, using human excrement for fuel."

How could God ask for such a thing? Why would God ask Ezekiel to turn human excrement into firewood?

God wanted to play out an example of contamination through Ezekiel's meal. If he baked the bread over human excrement, the bread would be soiled, distasteful.

The people during the time of Ezekiel were soiled with sin and distasteful in God's mouth. He wanted to spit them out, comparing their sin to human excrement.

We tend to see sin as a mistake, a common failure we all are guilty of, a little deviation from right that we need to correct.

God sees sin as human excrement. He hates it. Sure it's common and everybody's doing it, but that doesn't mean He has to like it. Sin revolts God.

This kind of doo-doo needs to be a don't-don't. Don't sin. Do obey God.

65. Ezekiel 5:10

Therefore in your midst parents will eat their children, and children will eat their parents. I will inflict punishment on you and will scatter all your survivors to the winds.

Cannibalism in the Bible? How disgusting? Is God for that?

No, God hates it, but the times in Ezekiel got so bad that it came down to parents eating their children and vice versa.

The threat of such action should have scared the people from ignoring God to following God obediently, yet it didn't. The people responded by saying "Not us. We would never do that." Yet they did.

The Bible talks about times during sieges around the city when food was cut off and the people turned to eating each other, even their own kids. Why did God allow things to get so desperate?

God always warned people that this would happen unless they confessed their sin and changed their ways. The people ignored Him and then realized He was right.

He's the God of *I-told-you-so*. He always gave plenty of warnings, but people never learn.

66. Ezekiel 24:16

"Son of man, with one blow I am about to take away from you the delight of your eyes. Yet do not lament or weep or shed any tears."

God told Ezekiel that his wife was going to die, then said not to cry at his wife's funeral. Harsh, huh?

As with everything God put Ezekiel through, God wanted to communicate something about his relationship with His people.

At the time, the people's relationship with God was on life support, near death. When it collapsed, God would not shed a tear. He had shed lots of them already. We see this kind of godly sorrow when Jesus cried over Jerusalem (Luke 19:41), longing to be close to them, yet they pushed Him far away.

God wanted Ezekiel to remain stoic at his wife's funeral just as God, after decades of trying, would remain emotionless at the collapse of Jerusalem. When the people saw Ezekiel react as he did over his wife, they had to wonder why and inquire about such behavior. This led to a sermon over their disobedience and an expression about God's disapproval of them.

God called Ezekiel to do a cold, harsh thing to bring up a cold, harsh reality.

67. Ezekiel 28:12-13

"Son of man, take up a lament concerning the king of Tyre and say to him: 'This is what the Sovereign LORD says:

"'You were the seal of perfection,
   full of wisdom and perfect in beauty.
You were in Eden,
   the garden of God...'"

Was the King of Tyre in the Garden of Eden? Impossible. That was a few thousand years before Ezekiel.

Ezekiel, in later verses, described the King in other terms, such as a cherub, blameless in his ways until wickedness took over and disgraced him before God. He was kicked to the earth.

This description sounds more like Satan and that was God's point when He communicated these thoughts to Ezekiel.

Satan was a magnificent angel, beautiful and smart, until his pride caused him to sin and God had to kick him out.

The city of Tyre, an island, sits on the Mediterranean (part of Lebanon today) and was a successful trade route which became very wealthy. God could be describing the King of Tyre specifically or Tyre as a city in Ezekiel, but either way, Tyre was beautiful, became prideful, and needed to face judgment for its sins.

Just like Satan.

68. Ezekiel 36:17

"Son of man, when the people of Israel were living in their own land, they defiled it by their conduct and their actions. Their conduct was like a woman's monthly uncleanness in my sight."

Okay, that's gross. Why would God talk about something like this? It seems inappropriate.

God used a gross metaphor to point out gross behavior.

According to Old Testament law (Leviticus 12), a woman's period made her unclean and she needed to be separated during that time. The touching of any blood, whether from a wound or a menstrual cycle, made someone unclean. Blood carried diseases and could contaminate another person.

Sin similarly spreads from person to person, contaminating them and defiling them. We shouldn't touch sin or be anywhere near. If we do, we cannot pass it on to our family.

Sin separates a holy God from His children. He hates sin and finds it detestable. It disgusts him. That's why this metaphor accurately describes His thoughts toward sin.

If you find this repulsive, then ask yourself, how do you see your own sin?

69. Ezekiel 44:18

They are to wear linen turbans on their heads and linen undergarments around their waists. They must not wear anything that makes them perspire.

Does God hate wool? Does he have a thing against cotton? Why is God so concerned about what kind of cloth the priests wore?

Linen appears more than silk, wool or cotton in the Bible (no polyester blends back then). Linens come from flax, made from plants. The strands of the plant are pulled apart separately and then woven together. These thinner strands are lighter than the other materials and cooler on the skin.

God made the other fabrics in this world for specific reasons, but He wanted linen for the priests. Why?

Priests worked hard, busily sacrificing animals around the clock. God didn't want them passing out due to heat exhaustion in the Middle East climate. The linen had a cleaner look to it and the priests needed to look presentable doing their bloody work. Maybe the linen cleaned up easier compared to other materials since the priests went home every night soaked in blood. Also, linen was a common material, not exotic like silk, reserved for kings and queens. These priests needed to identify more with the common man.

Everything about worship mattered to God, from the blueprints to the building to the design of the dress. Every detail means something to Him.

70. Daniel 7:20

I also wanted to know about the ten horns on its head and about the other horn that came up, before which three of them fell—the horn that looked more imposing than the others and that had eyes and a mouth that spoke boastfully.

Daniel had a vision of horns with eyes and mouths. So how does a horn talk? Did Daniel have too much spicy hummus for dinner?

In the Bible, a vision of a "horn" on a beast's head, represents a king in a kingdom. The beast (the kingdom) is bad and the horns that spread from the beast each give power to the beast's badness.

The horn of an animal represents its power. Little sheep with fluffy ears are not a threat. Rams and rhinos are.

So when Daniel dreamt about horns, God revealed to him the status of kings in one particular kingdom – how they will rise to power, how many there will be and how they will act.

This particular horn/king talked like a big show-off – "Look at me. It's good to be king!" – doing end zone dances and flexing his biceps.

While scholars debate the exact identities of Daniel's horns, we can know for sure the occupation of those horns – kings.

71. Hosea 1:2

When the LORD began to speak through Hosea, the LORD said to him, "Go, marry a promiscuous woman and have children with her, for like an adulterous wife this land is guilty of unfaithfulness to the LORD."

I thought God wanted us to be virgins before we marry? Why would he promote the marrying of a man to a prostitute?

First of all, we are all saved by grace. Our pasts can be forgiven and we can live with a new hope. This prostitute, Gomer, had a chance at a new life with a good man.

However, she slipped back into prostitution later and Hosea had to buy her out of her mistakes.

God wanted Hosea to marry her as an example. Like Gomer did to others, Israel prostituted herself with other gods and God needed to keep saving His people from their mistakes. As a prophet, Hosea experienced God's pain firsthand. He knew what it was like for his loved one to stray far away and show love to others.

God wants us to be virgins before we marry – pure and unsoiled. He also wants us to make Him the sole authority in our lives, never turning to any worldly thing for pleasure and purpose.

72. Jonah 4:2-3

He prayed to the LORD, "Isn't this what I said, LORD, when I was still at home? That is what I tried to forestall by fleeing to Tarshish. I knew that you are a gracious and compassionate God, slow to anger and abounding in love, a God who relents from sending calamity. Now, LORD, take away my life, for it is better for me to die than to live."

Jonah was a strange prophet. He didn't want to witness to the people of Nineveh so he ran away. God caused a storm on his ship, so Jonah jumped in the water and was saved by a big fish who transported him to the land. Jonah carried out the job and the entire city repented including the king.

By chapter 4, Jonah went to a mountain near Nineveh, presumably to watch the Sodom and Gomorrah fireworks show. When nothing happened, he complained, saying "I knew you were a good and loving God!"

Chill out, Jonah. Why so upset over God saving Nineveh?

Nineveh was the capital city of the Assyrian empire and they did some horrible things to people, including women and children. Jonah considered them an enemy and definitely showed prejudice (maybe justifiably) towards them.

Jonah was not a perfect prophet, but he showed something in us and our attitude towards our enemies. We may want them to be punished, before God can show them mercy. If we don't like that attitude in Jonah, we shouldn't like it in us.

73. Malachi 2:3

"Because of you I will rebuke your descendants; I will smear on your faces the dung from your festival sacrifices, and you will be carried off with it."

Did God just say He would smear poop on people's faces? Whoa.

He did. If you've ever had a dog and that dog had an accident in the house, you take the dog to the accident, point his nose at it and say "Look what you did! See the mess you caused! Never do that again!" You want to teach the dog a lesson.

Like a dog, we need lessons taught to us. Sometimes we have to have our noses pushed into it and be told "Look what you did! See the mess you caused! Never do that again!"

The religious festivals around the time of Malachi had been routine or self-indulgent. The people's hearts weren't into it or they were into it for the wrong reasons. God was angry. He had been through this before with the people and seen the separation and devastation it caused (two military giants toppled Israel and a third was in charge). God wanted them to return to the glory days, but sin was ruining that dream.

Sometimes God pushes our noses in our sinfulness and to see it for what it really is. Poo.

74. Matthew 5:5

"Blessed are the meek,
for they will inherit the earth."

Really? How do meek inherit the earth and do we want meek people taking over the earth? And what's so blessed great about being meek anyway?

The word *meek* in Greek means one with a mild, gentle spirit. Our world would be better off if we had mild-mannered, kind-hearted people ruling over us, instead of competitive, must-win, trample-on-the-backs-of-others-to-get-ahead types who make those all important decisions.

Jesus, in this section of the "Beatitudes," expresses a new way of thinking. In His kingdom, people who are mild and gentle get ahead in this world. In his kingdom, that kind of spirit is rewarded.

Jesus is telling us His kingdom operates differently than any kingdom on earth. In the Roman kingdom, power ruled. In Jesus' kingdom, meekness rules.

So it sounds counter-intuitive and it's supposed to. Jesus wants the peacemakers and persecuted to know He supports them.

75. Matthew 5:30

"And if your right hand causes you to stumble, cut it off and throw it away. It is better for you to lose one part of your body than for your whole body to go into hell."

That doesn't seem to be the best way to solve a sin problem. Cutting off body parts?

Think how many armless, footless, eyeless, earless people would be walking around—all of us! Productivity would decrease. We couldn't properly communicate, relate and connect with one another. All the handicapped parking would be gone!

But this is exactly how God sees us. We are all handicapped by sin. It sets us back and ruins our relationships. We can't do all that we were meant to do. Sins sets us back.

But this verse asks how important is it to you that you stop sin in your life. Would you be willing to sever a part of your body to prevent any more severing of your relationship with God?

God doesn't want you to mutilate yourself. He wants you to cut off those sinful areas of your life by choice and throw them away. It's more important that you are whole spiritually than physically.

76. Matthew 5:48

"Be perfect, therefore, as your heavenly Father is perfect."

Perfect? God wants us to be perfect? Yeah, good luck.

Perfection is, let's face it, impossible. Jesus was perfect, but c'mon, He's Jesus. The Son of God.

Perfection can only happen when all possible sin choices are gone from this life and all remnants of this selfish, habitual flesh have been eradicated.

So basically when we die, right, we'll be perfect?

Jesus wants us to act perfectly now, but He knows it's not possible. Yet, we can make perfection our goal. Yes, it's a command, but Jesus died for our sinful imperfection to help us accomplish that goal. So perfection is a possibility – a day-by-day choice to live like Jesus.

On the other hand, in God's eyes we are perfect, no marks of sin on our record since Jesus paid the price for all our imperfections. We commit sin, but receive forgiveness because of Jesus' sacrifice.

We will fail, but God has redeemed us and made us righteous in his eyes through Jesus' perfect resolution to our imperfection.

77. Matthew 6:8

"Do not be like them, for your Father knows what you need before you ask him."

So why pray if God already knows what I need?

This confusion comes from a misunderstanding of what prayer is all about. A parent loves to hear from a child no matter what they have to say. They love to hear what's going on in their child's life and hearing the heart of their child when they pray—what they like, what they hope for, what they need.

Prayer is a time of connection with God not to tell God what to do or to give God a checklist to make one's life easier. Prayer is conversation within a relationship. You talk to God because you love God and He loves you and wants to hear from you.

He wants to know what you need and hear it from your own lips. We do not throw our agenda at God and say "take care of it all" like He's some kind of super-assistant. Maybe in the process of talking it out with God you'll discover what's really important and what's not.

Don't pray thinking God already knows what you're going to say, so why bother. Pray knowing that God loves you and wants to hear from you no matter what you have to say.

78. Matthew 6:15

"But if you do not forgive others their sins, your Father will not forgive your sins."

So does my personal forgiveness depend on my ability to forgive? If that's the case, then is there someone on my list that I have not forgiven – some kid from my tenth grade class who tripped me in the lunch room – which means I am not forgiven?

In this statement, Jesus asked this question: if we ask God for forgiveness of our sins, yet we refuse to forgive others of their sins, then do we really understand forgiveness?

To truly understand forgiveness we must accept that we fall short of God's standard for our lives and that we are not perfect. We must apply that understanding of imperfection to others and forgive them too. If we don't, then we don't understand our own forgiveness.

To ask God not to expect perfection from us and yet we expect it from others is hypocritical. The gauge to monitor forgiveness in our lives centers on our ability to forgive others.

When one receives true forgiveness from God – honestly and transparently – then one humbly sees how cruel it is hold grudges against others. That person forgives like a child of God, acting like God and forgiving like God.

If we're forgiven, then we should forgive.

79. Matthew 12:32

"Anyone who speaks a word against the Son of Man will be forgiven, but anyone who speaks against the Holy Spirit will not be forgiven, either in this age or in the age to come."

Whoa, wait, there's an unforgiveable sin? No matter what I say or what I do...I'm doomed?

Jesus said this verse while talking to the Pharisees. They were guilty of continuous rejection of the Holy Spirit's prompting to accept the Messiah, Jesus, standing right before them. By rejecting the Holy Spirit's prompting, they were rejecting forgiveness which came through Jesus Christ. By rejecting the Holy Spirit, they were rejecting God. That's blasphemy.

The Holy Spirit's job is to convict us of sin so that we seek a savior from our sin. If we reject that we need a savior then we can't be saved...or forgiven.

So don't worry, we all reject the Holy Spirit, now and then, refusing to do the things that He nudges us to do.

But ongoing, continuous, around-the-clock rejecting of the Holy Spirit only leads to eternal doom. That's unforgiveable.

80. Matthew 16:4

"A wicked and adulterous generation looks for a sign, but none will be given it except the sign of Jonah." Jesus then left them and went away.

Of all the signs in the Bible, Jesus said that Jonah was the only sign? That's it? Aren't there more signs?

Jesus said this statement to individuals who wanted Him to perform tricks and do miraculous signs on the spot. Jesus could of, but He wasn't there to entertain them with only signs and miracles. He wanted them to grow in faith. That's why He asked some people about their faith before He healed them. It was not about someone getting physically better. It was about them getting spiritually better.

Jesus pointed to Jonah because Jonah was three days in the belly of a fish. Three days. Sound familiar? Jesus was three days in the grave. Jonah spent three days in fish-belly-hell. Jesus spent three days in a deep-dark-grave.

Jesus wanted the listeners to remember this sign so that when news spread of Jesus rising from the grave after three days, they would understand the clues.

That sign pointed to Jesus' power over the grave and His promise of a future resurrection for all believers.

81. Matthew 16:20

Then he ordered his disciples not to tell anyone that he was the Messiah.

What's the big secret? Why would Jesus tell people not to spread the news about him? I thought we were supposed to tell the world?

Jesus had a few motivations to ask people not to tell anyone He was the Messiah.

1. Timing: He wanted to keep the fervor about His arrival quiet so people wouldn't try to kill Him before Passover.

2. Misinformation: the disciples had only a partial view of who Jesus was. His resurrection was the final proof of His identity and they didn't have all that information yet.

3. Protection: Jesus cared for His disciples and didn't want them to get hurt spreading news that the religious leaders considered blasphemous.

Once Jesus resurrected, He gathered His apostles together and told them to go into the whole world and teach, baptize and disciple in His name. Jesus didn't want people to get ahead of themselves, but now there's no reason not to tell the world.

82. Mark 15:34

And at three in the afternoon Jesus cried out in a loud voice, *"Eloi, Eloi, lema sabachthani?"* (which means "My God, my God, why have you forsaken me?").

Did God the Father abandon Jesus on the cross?

It is impossible for the Father to separate himself from Jesus. The trinity is an impenetrable divine bond.

Jesus' cry came from His humanity on the cross. As the punishment for the sin of the world was laid on Him, Jesus felt the separation that comes from sin. He felt that separation for the first time, something He had not experience before because Jesus never sinned.

Also, a quick look at Psalm 22 which Jesus quoted in His cry, reveals a number of prophecies that were coming true before their eyes. It's like Jesus was saying, "Go home and read Psalm 22! You'll understand what's going on!" (There was no Psalm 22 since the Psalms weren't numbered then, but when Jesus said the line they immediately knew the rest.)

Jesus was not abandoned on the cross by His Father. He experienced the feeling of abandonment, but cried out this sentence so others would remember that God had not abandoned them. God had sent Jesus to earth to keep us from being separated from God forever.

83. Luke 11:24-26

"When an impure spirit comes out of a person, it goes through arid places seeking rest and does not find it. Then it says, 'I will return to the house I left.' When it arrives, it finds the house swept clean and put in order. Then it goes and takes seven other spirits more wicked than itself, and they go in and live there. And the final condition of that person is worse than the first."

Do demons "move in" to your brain? How do your keep your mind from being invaded by demonic squatters?

If someone leaves a house empty and never returns to maintain it, all kinds of creatures begin to move in. First it's the insects, spiders and cockroaches. Then it's the lizards, rodents and birds who eat the insects. Then the predators who eat the lizards, rodents and birds. Next thing you know the once empty house is full of unwanted creatures.

The same is true for our mind unless we constantly purify it with the word of God. Yes, kick Satan out of your head and be free of his influence, but if you don't move God in and routinely clean up the trash, spackle the holes and shoo away the evil, demonic influences will settle in and make themselves at home.

We are the landlords of our mind and we determine who lives there and who needs to be kicked to the curb.

84. Luke 12:51-53

"Do you think I came to bring peace on earth? No, I tell you, but division. From now on there will be five in one family divided against each other, three against two and two against three. They will be divided, father against son and son against father, mother against daughter and daughter against mother, mother-in-law against daughter-in-law and daughter-in-law against mother-in-law."

In this verse, doesn't Jesus seem okay with the fact that He's dividing families? Doesn't Jesus love families so why would He be okay with causing division?

Jesus doesn't want to divide families, but He recognizes that if someone believes in Him that not everyone in the family will be happy with that.

He came to show God's love and that unfortunately causes some to hate Him. Even our own family members.

Jesus needs to be the primary relationship in our life. Family, friends, spouses, children and bosses can't be more important than Him. Why? Because they sometimes selfishly demand our time and focus us away from what's truly important.

Jesus knows that if we focus on Him, He'll help us make all those other relationships more fulfilling and more meaningful. So He wants to help us love our families more, but in the right perspective.

85. Romans 5:20

The law was brought in so that the trespass might increase. But where sin increased, grace increased all the more...

Is the law causing sin? If that's the case, what good is it?

It's the fault of those speed limit signs that we speed, but try to convince the police officer of that. "Officer, if that speed limit sign wasn't there, I wouldn't be speeding." Good luck.

Paul was saying in Romans that as soon as laws were put into place, temptation increased. Once we knew the boundaries we wanted to cross them. Look at the Garden of Eden. One rule posted and Satan successfully got the first couple to break it. Suddenly that one fruit looked more appetizing than all the rest.

So laws do create the temptation to break them, but it's not the laws' fault. The laws create boundaries for our safety, warning us of upcoming pain. They are a good thing, but they inspire evil to do a bad thing.

Not only does temptation increase, but so does grace. God sees our disobedience and increases His forgiveness. Grace doesn't run out or reach a limit. God pours out more grace when needed.

Sin can try to separate us from God. It can't as long as God's grace supply never runs out.

86. Romans 7:19-20

For I do not do the good I want to do, but the evil I do not want to do—this I keep on doing. Now if I do what I do not want to do, it is no longer I who do it, but it is sin living in me that does it.

You lost me. What's Paul doing? Or not doing? Is he evil? Or good?

In Romans 7, Paul talks about the power of the law and the destructive nature of sin. The flesh, he acknowledges, does not naturally want to do good. The law points out that weakness in him. As soon as his flesh hears what God wants him to do, he immediately wants to do the opposite…to sin.

Paul laments over this tug of war inside him. He really wants to do good, but evil keeps pulling him in the other direction. He caves into the temptations and sins.

Paul does not find his identity in sin. It's not who he wants to be. Because Paul, in his heart, does not want to sin, then sin is the culprit. His identity is in Christ. To overcome this problem, Paul must understand the battle to win the war.

In these verses, Paul talked out the issue of what he spiritually wants to do and what his flesh sinfully wants to do. Instead of beating himself up, he confesses his weakness and acknowledges his desire – to do the right thing.

87. Romans 13:1-2

Let everyone be subject to the governing authorities, for there is no authority except that which God has established. The authorities that exist have been established by God. Consequently, whoever rebels against the authority is rebelling against what God has instituted, and those who do so will bring judgment on themselves.

Does God cause bad governments? Was God behind Nazi Germany and does He approve of the Taliban?

God allows governments to happen, giving the people what they want. The people desired the sins of a government and allowed those powers to have control over their lives. Then they suffered the consequences.

Can people rebel against those governments or must they just take what's coming to them? Dietrich Bonhoeffer and Corrie Ten Boom refused Hitler's tyranny. Many defied prejudices to bring freedom to blacks in America. Yes, we must speak out against that kind of injustice. Nazis, Taliban and the KKK are extremes though.

In our society, we may disagree with the government's position on abortion but we shouldn't bomb clinics. We may not like the President, but we can't pray for his death. We may not like how our tax money is spent, but we can't refuse to pay them.

The answer is not anti-government retaliation but pro-God communication to our government, backed by continued prayer.

88. Romans 14:2

One person's faith allows them to eat anything, but another, whose faith is weak, eats only vegetables.

Vegetarians are weak? Is this biblical proof to stay away from broccoli?

Paul speaks in Romans 14 about different places where people are in their faith. Some experience great freedom, knowing that they can eat a rare steak and not be breaking the old Jewish laws about consuming blood.

Others still hold on to certain traditions, feeling that food consumption ties in directly to their responsibility to take care of their bodies. They cannot let go of Old Testament laws and need those rules to help them experience their religion.

Paul simply acknowledges where people are in their walk. Some have progressed further down the road and others just aren't there yet.

We need to show grace to all of them – not criticizing the freer ones as liberal or labeling the law-abiders as ultra-conservative. God accepts everyone no matter where they are. He just doesn't want anyone to get stuck in one place, but always progressing to God's ideal for their lives.

89. 1 Corinthians 7:9

But if they cannot control themselves, they should marry, for it is better to marry than to burn with passion.

Should we marry only for reasons of passion? Is lust a justification to put a ring on it?

Paul spoke very frankly in 1 Corinthians 7 about people who were unable to control their sexual urges. So he challenges them…if you want the icing, then you have to take the cake. If you want the benefits, you have to do the work. It's a package deal. If you like sex, then get married.

Scare tactic? Maybe for some. Paul wanted to show the gravity of the sin. Commitment must accompany sex. Sex does not come free.

Touching a hot stove can seriously burn you. Messing with hot passion can burn you also. It clouds your judgment and bases your choice on purely physical reasons.

Self-control protects yourself and your relationship with God. A person must not take sex lightly or casually.

90. 1 Corinthians 7:15

For the unbelieving husband has been sanctified through his wife, and the unbelieving wife has been sanctified through her believing husband. Otherwise your children would be unclean, but as it is, they are holy.

Is the unbelieving husband saved by marrying a believer?

Unfortunately salvation does not work that way. Paul the apostle said that the husband was "sanctified." What does that mean?

Sanctified means to set aside for the purposes of God's glory. The believing wife brings God's purposes to the relationship. Her faith inspires and impresses on the husband and the children too. The husband is blessed by God by having a faithful wife. The children would be lost without that believing mother loving them and pointing them to God. The believing wife sets aside her family for something God wants to do with them—bring them all to Christ.

Marrying a Christian cannot save the unbelieving spouse, but it's hopeful that it will.

Salvation is about saying "I do" to Jesus Christ. Just as a person pledges his life to another in marriage, that person must pledge his or her life to Jesus Christ for what He has done for them, dying for their sins and promising an eternal relationship.

91. 1 Corinthians 7:38

So then, he who marries the virgin does right, but he who does not marry her does better.

How is not marrying a virgin a good thing? How is it better?

In 1 Corinthians 7, Paul the apostle made a case that it's better for someone to not marry and to serve the Lord instead. That was how Paul lived and it certainly worked for him.

Throughout this statement, Paul wanted to emphasize that giving your life to God was far better than giving yourself to marriage. A person's relationship with God is the most important relationship a person can have.

But, if one were to marry, marry a virgin, someone pure. Do not have sex before marriage and give yourself fully and solely to the one who you have committed yourself to.

If you're not married, don't be anxious. Emphasize your relationship with God and give that your full attention.

God loves you better than any spouse ever can. Serve Him with all that you have.

92. 1 Corinthians 14:34-35

Women should remain silent in the churches. They are not allowed to speak, but must be in submission, as the law says. If they want to inquire about something, they should ask their own husbands at home; for it is disgraceful for a woman to speak in the church.

Should churches tell women to shut up?

The story behind Paul's command to the Corinthian church has more to do with culture in their day. Women had a different role in first century society. They did not have the same rights. It was a male-dominant society so the church reflected some of those attitudes.

Does God look at women as second-class citizens? Absolutely not. Jesus Christ gave women more value than any other religion. He defended the women caught in adultery. He spoke to the Samaritan woman by the well. He listened to His mother. It was the group of women who discovered and announced His resurrection.

So should women honor this silence in churches today? Not necessarily. It wouldn't be appropriate for anyone to speak up in church. Church services are not audience participation. Hecklers are kicked out. Talkers are shushed.

Husbands and wives should talk about the service at home, sharing spiritual insight. Many churches today are blessed with female leadership, though other cultures may frown upon it.

Jesus was certainly counter-cultural and honored women greatly. A church today should do the same.

93. Hebrews 2:9

But we do see Jesus, who was made lower than the angels for a little while, now crowned with glory and honor because he suffered death, so that by the grace of God he might taste death for everyone.

Is Jesus lower than angels on the God scale?

Hebrews begins by explaining the theology behind Jesus coming to earth as a man. The idea of Him coming as fully God and fully man created confusion and caused many to twist theology to make that confusion work for them.

The writer of Hebrews wanted the reader to understand that Jesus came to earth fully man, for a period of time (around 33 years), in a human form that was one step below the angelic form. Jesus never lost His title or His status as God, but stepped off the throne (above angels) and to the earth (below angels).

Once Jesus died and resurrected, ascending into heaven, He retook the throne, which He technically never lost—just stepped away from temporarily—and returned to the place of glory and honor. Jesus needed to come to earth to taste/experience death so everyone could be freed from it.

Jesus made the angels. He could never be lower than them, but for a brief period in history He became man, humbling Himself to a place below heaven.

94. 1 Peter 3:19-20

After being made alive, he went and made proclamation to the imprisoned spirits—to those who were disobedient long ago when God waited patiently in the days of Noah while the ark was being built. In it only a few people, eight in all, were saved through water...

Did Jesus go to hell and hold a conference?

In chapter 3, Peter talked about Christians standing up for God and giving people a reason to believe. The Christian life, he said, will always be about suffering for doing good. Just like Jesus.

His death and resurrection confirmed the good news and destroyed evil's advances against God.

In these verses, Peter said that Jesus' resurrection proved that point to those who were dead, separated from God because of their sin, especially those all the way back to the days of Noah. Only eight people did the right thing and got on Noah's boat.

It says that proclamation occurred "after being made alive," after His resurrection, not after His crucifixion and burial. After three days in the grave, Jesus spent forty days on earth, then ascended in heaven. When did Jesus proclaim to the spirits in spirits in prison/hell? Hard to say. Jesus can do whatever He wants, wherever He wants. If He wanted to go to hell, He could. If He did, it was the greatest day hell would ever experience.

Peter wasn't interested in giving us Jesus' itinerary, but His purpose. Jesus' resurrection confirmed His victory and all of heaven and hell heard the news.

95. 1 John 3:6

No one who lives in him keeps on sinning. No one who continues to sin has either seen him or known him.

If I sin, am I not saved? Do I not know God if I sin?

We all sin, even Christians. A Christian "lives in him" meaning he has a relationship with God. A Christian invests his life in God and tries to live as Jesus would. Just because a Christian has a relationship with God, it doesn't mean he's impervious to outside influences and worldly temptations.

If someone "continues to sin" meaning he has no remorse or does not seek a way out of the sin, then it would come into question if the person has really encountered God. If that person claims to have a relationship with God, knows Jesus intimately from Scripture and has seen Him at work around him, why would that Christian keep on sinning?

A Christian will sin but, with the guidance of the Holy Spirit living in him, he won't continue to sin. He'll repent from that sin and fight that sin from becoming a major issue in his life.

Thankfully Jesus' sacrifice forgives all past, present and future sin. His grace keeps cleansing us from sin. Our sin is not held against us and wiped away. If a Christian "lives in him" and keeps his life close to Jesus, he will not sin.

96. 1 John 5:6

This is the one who came by water and blood—Jesus Christ. He did not come by water only, but by water and blood. And it is the Spirit who testifies, because the Spirit is the truth.

How did Jesus come by water and blood? Water and blood were consistent themes in Jesus' time on earth.

Jesus Christ came to earth as the God-man—fully God and fully man. He came by water as witnessed by his birth, as any human would, developed in the amniotic sac of Mary and delivered into this world. At the birth, He entered the world with water and blood as part of the delivery process.

Jesus announced His identity and ministry at his baptism, in the waters of the Jordan River where God spoke and the Holy Spirit descended.

Jesus allowed Himself to be killed on the cross, coming as a sacrifice for the forgiveness of all sins. His blood was shed to fulfill the sacrificial requirements outlined in the Old Testament. When the Roman guard pierced Jesus to finalize His death, water and blood spilled out (John 19:34).

Jesus called Himself the Water of Life to the woman at the well. Whoever drank of Him would never go thirsty. At the Last Supper, Jesus communicated how His blood gives everyone who believes eternal life, redeeming sinners from their sin and cleansing them of all unrighteousness.

It is through these elements of water and blood that Jesus communicated His message and fulfilled His purpose

97. Jude 9

But even the archangel Michael, when he was disputing with the devil about the body of Moses, did not himself dare to condemn him for slander but said, "The Lord rebuke you!"

Was there a fight over Moses' body? Where was this in the Old Testament?

Good question. This is a mysterious reference in a small book of the New Testament. Until people read this verse, they knew nothing about this incident. So where did Jude come up with it?

The author of Jude was one of Jesus' earthly brothers. The Gospels say His brothers struggled with His deity (understandable) but eventually came to believe in Him. So did Jesus talk about this around the dinner table and Jude made note of it.? Don't think so.

Jude wrote in his short letter about the ungodly slipping into the churches and causing disruption. He warned of angels who fell under temptation and left to follow Satan. Towns like Sodom and Gomorrah did the same by falling into sin. These people rejected authority and slandered whenever they could.

Jude wanted to make the point that even the archangel Michael wouldn't say anything out of line or speak beyond what was appropriate even if Michael were talking to Satan and saying "The Lord rebuke you." The Lord rebukes Satan, but Michael would be careful in saying the same thing.

This is one interpretation that people have gotten from this. Every now and then, a verse in the Bible is mysterious, but it does have a plausible explanation.

98. Revelation 4:8

Each of the four living creatures had six wings and was covered with eyes all around, even under its wings. Day and night they never stop saying:
"'Holy, holy, holy
is the Lord God Almighty,'
who was, and is, and is to come."

Doesn't Revelation sound like crazy mythology? Multi-winged creatures with eyes?

The book of Revelation, written by John, is very different in its design from other books. Two books are like it – Ezekiel and Zechariah, both written by prophets who had visions that needed explanation.

Scholars call these *apocalyptic* books, which means *messages that were unknown which are now being revealed.* Revelation and the other books reveal strange messages that have a hidden meaning. The four living creatures in this verse are angels who had wings. They were earlier described as four-part creatures – lion, ox, man, eagle – saying they had qualities of each, not that they were some kind of bizarre minotaur.

These angels have six wings, two to cover their feet, two to cover their faces and two to fly. Covering feet and face are signs of humility, showing respect in the presence of God. They have many eyes, meaning they see what's going on around the world and in all directions. Like a fly, you can't sneak up on them.

So everything in Revelation is meant to be fantastic and outlandish, but it all has a real down-to-earth meaning. Revelation glimpses into heaven and it's really saying that the experience can't be described in terms we easily understand.

99. Revelation 20:14

Then death and Hades were thrown into the lake of fire. The lake of fire is the second death.

How is death thrown into a fiery lake?

As Revelation closes, God pronounces judgment on the things that will no longer be in the eternal world. Heaven will not be a place of crying, pain and suffering. There's no more death. Death is put to death.

So two things get tossed out – death and Hades (which represents the grave). Hades is not Hell, because the lake of fire represents that.

God shows us that one day will come when we no longer have to dress in black and read eulogies. Funeral homes go out of business. Nobody will play Taps ever again. Grave stones disintegrate and obituaries disappear.

Death and the grave die a second death, a spiritual death, separating them from the living for eternity.

The funeral of death will be the last funeral all believers will ever attend. And nobody will be crying.

100. Revelation 22:7

"Look, I am coming soon! Blessed is the one who keeps the words of the prophecy written in this scroll."

How soon is soon and why hasn't Jesus come back yet?

The word "soon" in Revelation is controversial. Some think Jesus meant that He's already come back. Some think He came back and He's living on earth right now. Others think He'll come back tomorrow while others presume it's in the distant future.

The answer is nobody knows when He's coming back and those that say they do are not following God's word. So why did Jesus say "soon" and not "some time"?

"Soon" indicates urgency. If parents tell a child that they are coming home soon, the child is on alert and is more obedient. If they tell that child they'll be home in a couple days, all kinds of temptations creep in. Jesus wants us to be on our toes, living as if He's coming back today.

When Jesus does return, it will feel quick, suddenly without warning. So "soon" describes the feeling those will experience when He does.

If Jesus returned tomorrow, two thousand years after this Revelation was spoken, it would seem like "soon" especially when viewed in light of eternity. For God, a day is like a thousand years (2 Peter 3:8), so in that sense Jesus was really saying "I'll be back in a couple days." That's soon.

Jesus is coming soon, much sooner then when He first said this, and every day He waits, we only have more opportunities to serve Him.

The 100 Most Confusing Bible Verses Index

Number of verses from each book
- Genesis – 26
- Exodus – 4
- Leviticus – 5
- Numbers – 2
- Deuteronomy – 3
- Joshua – 1
- Judges – 3
- 1 Samuel – 1
- 2 Samuel – 4
- 1 Kings – 1
- Job – 1
- Psalms – 2
- Proverbs – 1
- Ecclesiastes – 3
- Song of Songs – 1
- Isaiah – 1
- Jeremiah – 2
- Ezekiel – 8
- Daniel – 1
- Hosea – 1
- Jonah – 1
- Malachi – 1
- Matthew – 8
- Mark – 1
- Luke – 2
- Romans – 4
- 1 Corinthians - 4
- Hebrews – 1
- 1 Peter – 1
- 1 John – 2
- Jude – 1
- Revelation – 3

The 100 Most Confusing Bible Verses in Order

1. Genesis 1:4
2. Genesis 1:27
3. Genesis 2:9
4. Genesis 2:22
5. Genesis 3:1
6. Genesis 3:7
7. Genesis 3:9
8. Genesis 4:15
9. Genesis 5:5
10. Genesis 6:4
11. Genesis 6:6
12. Genesis 9:24-25
13. Genesis 11:9
14. Genesis 14:18
15. Genesis 19:4-5
16. Genesis 19:8
17. Genesis 19:26
18. Genesis 19:31-32
19. Genesis 20:12
20. Genesis 22:2
21. Genesis 25:34
22. Genesis 26:8-9
23. Genesis 29:28
24. Genesis 32:28
25. Genesis 38:9-10
26. Genesis 42:8
27. Exodus 7:3-4
28. Exodus 20:7
29. Exodus 33:20
30. Exodus 34:14
31. Leviticus 4:2
32. Leviticus 11:10
33. Leviticus 19:19
34. Leviticus 24:14
35. Leviticus 26:18
36. Numbers 22:28

The 100 Most Confusing Verses of the Bible

37. Numbers 23:19
38. Deuteronomy 5:9
39. Deuteronomy 7:3
40. Deuteronomy 22:5
41. Joshua 6:21
42. Judges 6:39
43. Judges 11:39
44. Judges 16:19
45. 1 Samuel 28:13-14
46. 2 Samuel 1:15
47. 2 Samuel 2:2
48. 2 Samuel 10:4
49. 2 Samuel 24:13
50. 1 Kings 11:3
51. Job 1:8
52. Psalm 61:4
53. Psalm 98:8
54. Proverbs 25:21-22
55. Ecclesiastes 1:2
56. Ecclesiastes 7:3
57. Ecclesiastes 10:19
58. Song of Songs 4:2
59. Isaiah 64:6
60. Jeremiah 13:4
61. Jeremiah 31:29
62. Ezekiel 1:10
63. Ezekiel 1:16
64. Ezekiel 4:12
65. Ezekiel 5:10
66. Ezekiel 24:16
67. Ezekiel 28:12-13
68. Ezekiel 36:17
69. Ezekiel 44:18
70. Daniel 7:20
71. Hosea 1:2
72. Jonah 4:2-3
73. Malachi 2:3
74. Matthew 5:5

75. Matthew 5:30
76. Matthew 5:48
77. Matthew 6:8
78. Matthew 6:15
79. Matthew 12:32
80. Matthew 16:4
81. Matthew 16:20
82. Mark 15:34
83. Luke 11:24-26
84. Luke 12:51-53
85. Romans 5:20
86. Romans 7:19-20
87. Romans 13:1-2
88. Romans 14:2
89. 1 Corinthians 7:9
90. 1 Corinthians 7:15
91. 1 Corinthians 7:38
92. 1 Corinthians 14:34-35
93. Hebrews 2:9
94. 1 Peter 3:19-20
95. 1 John 3:6
96. 1 John 5:6
97. Jude 9
98. Revelation 4:8
99. Revelation 20:14
100. Revelation 22:7

The 100 Most Confusing Verses of the Bible

ABOUT THE AUTHOR

Troy Schmidt began writing animation in Los Angeles in 1985 (Dennis the Menace, Heathcliff, Flintstone Kids). In 1992, he moved to Orlando to write for The Mickey Mouse Club, for three seasons. He adapted a Max Lucado children's book Hermie into a video, then created and wrote all the future video installments and twenty Hermie books. Troy directed documentary footage in Israel for iLumina Gold, then returned in 2008 to host a documentary entitled "In His Shoes: The Life of Jesus" for GLO Bible software. Troy was also a producer for the GSN game show "The American Bible Challenge" starring Jeff Foxworthy and wrote the board game based on the show.

Troy is married to Barbie and they have three grown boys. He is a campus pastor at First Baptist Church Windermere, Florida.

BOOKS

Fish Sandwiches: The Delight of Receiving God's Promises (NavPress)

Revealed: Discovering Your True Identity in Christ for Teen Boys and Young Men (B&H Kids)

NIV Kid's Quiz Bible (Zondervan)

Bible Trivia, Jokes & Fun Facts for Kids (Bethany House)

The Extreme Old/New Testament Bible Trivia Challenge (Broadstreet)

The Best 100 Bible Verses About Prayer (Bethany House)

The Best 100 Bible Verses About Heaven (Bethany House)

The 100 Most Encouraging Verses of the Bible (Bethany House)

This Means War: A Prayer Journal (B&H Kids)

The American Bible Challenge Daily Reader: Volume 1 (Thomas Nelson)

The 100 Most Confusing Verses of the Bible

Chapter by Chapter: An Easy to Use Summary of the Entire Bible (Amazon)

Reason for Hope: Answers to Your Bible Questions (Amazon)

Reason for Hope: MORE Answers to Your Bible Questions (Amazon)

Reason for Hope: Answers to Your Questions about Heaven (Amazon)

40 Days: A Daily Devotion for Spiritual Renewal (Amazon)

Saved: Answers That Can Save Your Life (Amazon)

Release: Why God Wants You to Let Go (Amazon)

In His Shoes: The Life of Jesus (Amazon)

Laughing Matters (Lillenas Publishing)

Foundations: A Study of God (Amazon)

Living the Real Life: 12 Studies for Building Biblical Community (Amazon)

HOLDING THE LINE: AMERICA'S FIGHT FOR RELIGIOUS FREEDOM

The first freedom the Founding Fathers listed before all the other freedoms was religious liberty. Why? They knew that when the first one crumbled, all the rest would follow too. That's because they believed religious freedom was given to us by God—"endowed by their Creator with certain unalienable rights." They vowed that Congress could not establish a religion nor prohibit anyone from exercising their faith.

The separation of church and state movement today threatens that first liberty. Join Troy as he examines where these freedoms came from and argues what will happen if atheists cross the line. Written to encouraged Christians to hold that line of freedom in America.
               (Available only on Amazon)

FISH SANDWICHES:
THE DELIGHT OF RECEIVING GOD'S PROMISES

We all have this in common: We get hungry. Inevitably, we eventually notice something we lack, and we wonder how we're going to get our needs met. And then sometimes we notice that someone else has already taken care of our needs. And then sometimes we notice that the One who is taking care of our needs is God.

This warm and down-to-earth book invites you to sit in on one of the most miraculous moments of human history, when one Man took a few fish and a couple of loaves of bread and fed an entire village. Meet the Jesus who dares you to ask Him to give you each day your daily bread, who makes promises and keeps them, and who does immeasurably more than you can ask or imagine on a regular basis.

Made in United States
Orlando, FL
05 September 2023